The Bird You Are

The Bird You Are

LISA DART

SHANGANA PRESS

Published by
Shangana Press
Portland, Oregon, USA
shanganapress.com

ISBN: 979-8-9871359-4-5 (paperback)
ISBN: 979-8-9871359-5-2 (eBook)

Library of Congress Control Number: 2025941018

to and for my mother
Janet May Dart (née Graham)
15 July 1928 – 27 April 2019

Contents

SEAGULL

Chekhov's play taught me about you. Though it's not his seagull I have in mind now, but one we saw once, Mum, do you remember, caught in an incoming tide? The wash of wave by the wood groyne taking the bird under in a grey-white-feathered tidal flush. Recovering just enough to raise its head, find its feet. Too wet and dizzy to escape before the next wave rushed it down. "I feel like that seagull," you said, the day after Dad's funeral. I looked across at you. Bowed over, your brow crumpling, your pale eyes, tears, your mouth's fine lines, hard-fletched. You were in that black, quilted jacket. The crisscross stitching meant to plump the diamond pattern, already fraying. Bunched up in your jacket, hunched at the far end of the settee by the gas fire, two awkward pillows behind your collapsed back, you sat there wearing it for the whole day, day in, day out. And even when splattered by the food you ate (with your fingers, infant-like, the plate precarious) and I said I'd wash it, you refused to take it off, pulled it all the more close. In the play, Masha says what you couldn't. "I am in mourning for my life." You wore that jacket for the next few years, till it split. Odd parts of inner stuffing beginning to tell — white feathers poking through. And, though sea-soaked, you always wore it zipped, to hold back the tide, its ruthless undertow. To just about keep your head up. Stop your heart from breaking through.

TIME PAST AND TIME PRESENT

I can't quite get so far back in childhood to separate it all. In my mind, there's snow on the roses and the summer sun on pastel yellows, pinks, oranges. You're the bird that's there. Everywhere. Singing. Nesting. Hanging out sheets spun in some old machine, bundled in your plastic laundry basket. Solid, unforgettable, like a huge colander on the lawn. But there's also snow, your fur coat, sheepskin boots, and my Dad's gone. How can both be true? This summer, so many years further on, in the day-to-day months of heat, how the roses bloom. Last Saturday, I'd been out, come back, stared at, most of all, a single rose. Its petals yellow and thin-lined red. Striped as if with blood. Then I went, the shutters shuttered down, to the cool of my room. Alive in me, the small child I was, weeping: I lost you, Mum, in the snow's cold. Though somehow, you're still there in the garden sun. Your hair's red. Dulled-white sheets on the line. The air — rose-scented, warm.

FLIGHT

I am thinking of things we couldn't say, the long migration from the facts of what happened with my Dad, those very many years before he died. Our hearts rusted from the inside out. Take the word *flight:* moving through the air with wings. A plane, but also a bird of course. And a metaphor: to take flight, run away. But when it comes to the mind — its pushings off, the going further, losing it: guilty/gilty metals in dark dreams, blinding silver glints, hands wrung, candles guttering, slumbery agitation through the night — where are the words for what's corroded us? Delving down to define, loosen soil, root up, I also uncover in the O.E.D. *flight:* abhorrence *of;* shrinking *from,* and by the way and for example, in no particular order: father, sword, blood, husband, throat.

WAITING

I only know I'm four or five and I'm on a chair in the school's entrance hall. The other children — bustlers first, then the stragglers, the kids who'd thought they'd lost their shoe bag, satchel, the one who couldn't find a cap, but then retrieved it, laughing, calling, waving at, their hand held to go home — have long since echoed out. My legs are paled, cold, my feet in Clark's broad, brown sandals, diamond cuts in the front, the morning's hurried-on ankle socks no longer warm enough. The summer's early sun has changed to black cloud which, by late afternoon, might storm down rain. In the pocket of my zebra dress, the You-must-eat-it last of the school dinner I couldn't face. Marbles on the grass at lunchtime are the brightest things. Blue, red, or green, a perfected swirl of desire, frozen, untouchable through the glass. You haven't come. How long is it? How many days did it go on? I recall only the heart-beat glimmerings of hope, someone's footsteps, then how desolation swings, blade-like, through the doors — just a teacher, What are you doing here alone? A kind consternation, but I can hardly stammer something out, because one of us will think, my mother's late, she doesn't care, has let me down. I don't want to pull up the words, hear them shaped on my tongue. I won't let myself think the monstrous things: my dad's in hospital, she's forgotten me. Will never come. Why don't you move over here, then you can see the fish? And so I am left to green and gold flickering. The glass is marble-clear, the air pump bubbles on. A huge heart, out of body, swims through the silent weeds — bereft and black.

YOUR VERSION

Last night my dream, a train journey in India. Boundaries everywhere were gone. Through the windows such colours, palette strong — red, orange, blue, green. Before I'd slept, I wondered how I'd tackle the thing that must be looked at next: Dad's slash to his own throat. But this dream was so gentle, just a train's slow chug through the countryside. The only anxious bit: I hadn't had inoculations, but then a needle and a serum don't protect against the things I couldn't speak. This morning, I sifted the mind's wanderings about what you'd told me, Mum, how it had been: "I called the ambulance. No-one cried, we were all too shocked. I went with your dad to the hospital. You were four, hadn't even started school, didn't really understand... ." But I knew you had taken me across the road that Saturday to the colonel's house. In the hall, brought back from India, the foot of an elephant made into an umbrella stand. I stared speechless. How could anyone do such a thing? And my father too, sword in hand, doing what he did?

YOUR COAT

Most of all, I loved that beaver lamb. Brown, thick, so heavy, as a child I could hardly lift it. You wore it with those ankle boots, brown, sheepskin, zipped up. Commuters had already flattened down the snow, the mile or more along Tubbenden Lane into town. The path, foot-printed, took us to the railway bridge, bricks black from the traffic, the station round the corner, across the road and up the hill. The war memorial, down the other way into Orpington, the high street shops. Mum, did we walk, snow piled high on either side, pure white, grimed black on the edge, because Dad was in hospital, and the firm had come to take the car? And was it just once or many times? Your boots, their soles unbending, an onward, matt, flat step through unending snowed-down cold.

HOW IT SEEMED

Once, on a TV documentary, writhing, held down to calm his fit, a boy, bitten by some sort of foreign fox. The child I was, I took in everything, got it all mixed up. You worked for Supplementary Benefit. (The place you went to for help when Dad had gone to hospital and things were tough. They told you, so your story goes, put your kids in an orphanage, get a job.) Back from one of the home visits you had to make, demon-driven, you didn't speak, took off your jacket, shoved it in the washing machine. One pale hand seized the washing up bowl, the other grabbed, shaped in to it, the outlet hose. I didn't understand exactly what happened when you went to people's homes, how anyone could quantify the hand to mouth of need. I just watched as the machine chugged, drummed and shook. And you seemed relieved, a good job done, a crisis passing, when the machine spewed out dirt-black swirling soapsuds. Finally, you spoke: "There's cancer in the house I went to this afternoon…I could smell it." I watched the machine disgorge the diseased, the dark, the dank. Our lives about to overflow with rabid froth.

A PHOTOGRAPH

Of course, there is that one picture everyone remembers and wanted once they'd moved away. Recently, my niece in Australia, "Do you have that picture of Grandma, the one she kept on her dressing table?" You're seventeen, hair like Rita Hayworth's. (Back then, over here, American soldiers whistled, called to you across the street, "How ya doing, Red?") The bow of your lips, strongly curved, is lipsticked in vermillion. The colour, made from cinnabar, speaks of life, blood, eternity. Your skin is smooth, alabastered, camera-lit. Your eyes the lightest blue. Sometimes, even now at 90, they have that same distance, the same strange expectancy. But the picture's a relic of the time, a film star look-a-like, too stylised. Although I'm always shocked by beauty — you're heart-throb glamorous in a suit, hair brushed off your forehead, thick red waves down the black — there's another picture I prefer. You're in a belted coat with your parents on Paignton sea-front, perhaps you're about ten or twelve. I like it for all your freckles. Their smudgy day-to-dayness: the presence of the girl I still see, sometimes, in the white-haired woman you now are. And for the way you're looking out, the wings in your step.

THE WAY IT GOES

A girl in the film *How to Make An American Quilt* is high up on the rock. The day is beautiful, her first beloved near, though out of sight. Her body's tanned, slim, muscular. She's stretching into the light. Is it there, that second, the camera takes the heart? Or is it as her heels lift and fall, a pulsing prep for what comes next? Perhaps it's when she turns for a second's surety to see he's watching. Then, tipping her body slightly over, arms out front, she springs up arrow-straight, believes her future's flashing forth. A glittering weapon of fleshed intent, diving in, she breaks the lake's blue possibilities into white. Or is it later (after married years, children, her husband's long distance work, foreign affairs) in the new-build quiver of her house, she's looking out from an upstairs window, when he lifts, as a surprise, the plastic cover on a small garden pond. Mum, we know this girl from inside, those silent, frantic strokes. Both of us longed for words, their high dives in the day, the day's light, but madness left us to drown in the dark, the deep. The film's run on — underwater, flailing, our mouths bubble. We cannot speak.

EDWARD HOPPER'S PICTURE OF YOU

This must have been when the clocks went back. I'd stopped at the level crossing for a train. The train's length meant the London one — Hopper-lit, waiting to go through. The evening black, the lights, icon-bright, already on. And I saw you sitting by a carriage window, alone and calm. How come? You nearly always used the car. Such a strange coincidence both of us in the same place at the same time. And I waved trying to get your attention. You won't know the painting I was reminded of, though the woman in it with a magazine has your red hair. And next to her unexpected yellow hand-holds for opening the window, getting some air, calling out. The view from the painted train is somewhat uncertain, there could be snow on the ground, though up too close, untempered, winter-black, those leaf-bare trees. Their darkest depths, a place you went to all the time. Your suit, your hat and hatband, all three, fashioned painterly, completely black. But you're sitting there in the train, more elegant, smart, poised than you ever seemed to me — Hopper's brushed-up your mood swings, ragings, unending envies, unspoken grief. And hasn't he caught your legs well? Now, as so often, you're looking away from me at something else, disturbance sulking in the ceiling, the compartment's sides. But far off, the lighter colours in the sky, yellow, orange, mauve hold hope — that you will see me. There could be another painting of *Compartment C*, where Hopper's put that black mute wood in bespoke greens to catch the spring sunlight; where you'll wave back, come to the window, smash the wintered glass, put the clocks forward, raise the barrier between us.

YOUR COAT

As we went to the town, did you say anything? Tell me what'd happened would come right? And, of course, it wasn't as simple as you later said, "Driving, actually, he was backing up, the kind of winter you wouldn't believe how cold." And I imagined all too easily the snow-dark lane, the black night's white. My father driving, turning round. "He hit his head, that's what started it… we'd always been very happy." How could you or I understand it then the barrelled bullet of gunned up grief firing out another way? His mother's death when he was nine, alone then to boarding school. When we got back, you put your boots, upside down on the mat. Snow rigid in the tread took so long to melt and, even so, brought coldness everywhere. I've come to understand my hard-to-leave and go my own way, wanting still, somewhere, that small-child warmth: your beaver lamb. As we walked, one of my hands enfolded, where your elbow bent, in the folds of fur.

INHERITANCE

In your hand a spray of forsythia from your father's garden.
You're bending down with a trowel, the dark earth breaking up.
The forsythia I described in a poem as 'spring's bright filament.'
A connection to all that mattered. The garden's rich with
raspberry canes, holly, pear trees, roses and this forsythia...Was
this after or before the bad things that happened happened?
The petal after petal of my childhood years unfolding, falling
on pavement slabs, takes me today to a therapist. In a few
moments, I will knock on the black front door, enter her cool
green room, talk of my father — his actions wild, his thoughts
untrellised. But sitting on a street wall waiting, the flagrant fall
of flowers on concrete makes me think of you.

HYDRANGEAS

Their colours tyrannise. In the sharp stasis of summer sun, white or pink or blue or even, sometimes, pink and blue on the same stem. A kind of madness, a split identity, not knowing quite who or what one is. Blown up, bigger than other English flowers, somehow suburban, somehow mysterious. Their moody petals — you.

IF I COULD PAINT

you, it would be on the beach. From my mind's blue rise and fall, suffused with salt air and sun, would be another picture Hopper might have caught. Certainly he'd paint the rushing tide, the breaking white. A paper bag would be somewhere off centre, small, a smudge, far away, an obscure detail really (top right?). You've bought us hot pasties and your hands, sandy, sun-freckled, elegant, have torn the bag, let out the heat. Your thighs would be white and flesh-toned, you're running into the sea. Your shoulders though, Ambre-Solaired, two weeks a year (often rainy) to get them sun-bronzed, and there would be us applying it, each to the other, us getting on. Streaked in a maddening yellow, daubed through everything: your stomach's skin-puckered stretch marks beneath that white bikini and, there could be, thickly painted, a swirling smear to lather in, the reassurance, love, fun, somewhere there, always, with the scent of suncream. Gulls, in their high, air-drift circlings would be fine, single brush marks, for your sense of the spiritual that, when it comes, nearly always takes me unaware. The waves are shallow, the wind is scattering foam and you're shrieking as I splash you, dive, swim off, though turning back, never losing sight of you. How could I? You're in that ditsy-daisy swimming hat! The one — do you remember — how we both laughed when you put it on?

NOTHING'S PERFECT

I still have that cinnabar bracelet you gave me. It wasn't gold or silver like most of the things you bought to sell and, as you said, "I can't wear it, not with my hair." The bracelet was a paradox, an intricately carved design, an orange-red round simplicity. "What is cinnabar exactly, Mum?" You said, "I think it's a resin." But like so many things you told me, I wondered, if that was right? I've looked up the word, wanting a colour to describe an Indian sari and, in *that* photograph, a seventeen-year old's hard-won red lipstick. Cinnabar, or cinnabarite: the merchant's stone, a sulphide (HgS), comes from mercury. But merchant though you were, you didn't know this. The stone's associates: hot springs, volcanoes. Things that — your hair said it all — conjure temper tantrums, the raging days, the poison you directed everywhere. The word *mercury* comes from the Greek and there's a health warning in most write-ups: be careful when handling cinnabar, any mercury might affect the skin. And I'd add sometimes, in extreme cases, the heart.

KEEPSAKES

In Greece last year, I walked through the Church of a Hundred Doors, the oldest in Byzantium. Sun on the white of its facade, columns, courtyard, carved marble fountain. But it was in the toilets, being Sunday and over-used, I thought of that scarab charm you let me have. Gold, 18 carat. Back at home, trying as always to connect with you, I said, "I like it most, small and beautiful as it is, because the scarab's a symbol of eternity." Denying your always, in potentia, sensibility, you made me wince, laugh: "It's a dung beetle, really. And remember, Lees, where there's shit, there's always money." Later I had the cameo. And you surprised me as you sometimes did, with your knowledge. "It's Leda and the Swan, isn't it?" You'd left school at fourteen and seldom ever read anything. I wondered how you knew, but didn't ask. I wanted it because of the myth as well as the beauty of the thing. But how much did you know about Zeus, Yeats, the allusion to the fall of Troy or the white rush of moment by moment experience — the consciousness we humans have? How time's slowed and stilled in the finest, telling shapes of art? I look at it now: the milky-white figures, exquisitely carved, the translucent caramel background with simple safety chain and 9 or 14 carat gold surround. Hold and turn for the white of wings, Leda's skin, the violent, tender passions in the bird you are.

BUYING

Now I am remembering flea markets over forty years ago. All the ones we roamed and rummaged round. Clothes, rings, paintings, bric-a-brac. Beckenham, Petticoat Lane, Bromley. And Brighton — early on a Saturday. A tawdry, dawn sky, a field's low cold mist eventually traded-in for sun. How you loved those early mornings, those Brighton streets. And picking up and putting down, haggling. Your milieu becoming mine. We ate an early breakfast at a small cafe we nicknamed "Tiffany's": scrambled eggs, toast, coffee. After all the buying done, the good stuff, nearly always in need of polishing, tucked away in a pocket or little purse. Your deft fingers told me what you often later said, "I can make on that". And you did, with your own stall once a week. One Sunday at the care home, a pause between us and, suddenly really looking at me you simply whispered, not apropos of anything, nor literary at all, though it made my heart ring, "Breakfast at Tiffany's".

YOUR CLOTHES

hung around on doors, walls, a glass-fronted cabinet. You insisted on this, to keep a paranoid eye on things. Upstairs, where now you couldn't go (living downstairs, a tv, one room, adjustable bed, a commode) in all three bedrooms, wardrobes spilt, only half-closed, drawers, brim-filled, overflowed. Other stuff lay around in piles, jumpers, skirts, trousers, suits. Folded on hangers, hung in and outside wardrobe doors, all the outfits you put together over years: whites, browns, creams, caramels, all the shades there are of green, planning, one day, of walking out in linens, mohair, cashmere, silks. (You also bought, couldn't help yourself: nylon, viscose, polyester, the harsher brights of acrylic). You dressed me in them too when I was a child, for economy and, as if I was you.

HOSPITAL, ME

My hair is brown. So it was obvious to me, I wasn't from the same unpolished, rough-cut as you. But I didn't know I had another self buried further down, a deeper vein — that raging was all but hereditary. Like that cinnabar bracelet, another kind of heirloom which burst out from the darkest mine of unmined things. I screamed at my therapist when, out of it, I thought she was you, had let me down. When you came to hospital to visit me, walking with one of those wheelie things I'd nicknamed your trolley bus, the effort to do so killing, I told you right away to go. So, perhaps, because you said many times, "Nothing in life is ever perfect, Lees," I've kept the bracelet, though it's chipped. Besides, the colour never fails to draw my eye and, more than this, it has an odd kind of grace. It reminds me when in the hospital, wild with an anger I didn't know I had, I saw, and still do now, how hard it was for you to walk towards me, though you did. Blood pressure and love cinnabarred across your face.

YOUR DOPPY SHOES

Rubber soles. Well-worn leather. I'd always called them your *doppy* shoes. And now I wonder about that word. What exactly does it mean? I never really knew, but liked to use it. An intimacy. Especially as you aged and I would call in once a week to take you out. We couldn't find any other shoes to fit. So you had to wear them with everything, whatever skirt, whichever place. You had what the doctor called *bilateral oedema*. And your feet were red, fat, bulging under the pulled-tight front strap. I called them *doppy* as if I were the child, the one that might have a tantrum anytime, a flight of fury, a mad switch and, once dressed, would rage as you often did, "No! No! I am not going out!" even though you'd put those shoes on. After your first stroke I bought you other shoes — you screamed for them on the hospital phone, "Get them now, today, from the disabled shop in Eastbourne, you're stopping my recovery, holding me back." One of the nurses called them your moon boots and that made you laugh. Specially designed, open-toed, adjustable, extra wide. Even so you couldn't do them up yourself. And I knew how you envied all the girls with pink, red and orange statement heels, the skinny jeans over slender legs to set them off. But I always liked to ask if I should get your doppy shoes, knowing, whatever the word meant, no-one else would call them that. *Doppy: extremely clumsy, goofy, different, weird, funny.* The leather, white, kept us going with its stretch. The give — our stepping rhythm, a mother-daughter, daughter-mother yield.

YOUR PERFUMES

Clearing your bedroom, I found fifteen bottles of perfume, years old, some half-filled, others never opened, still in "posh-store" cellophane: Giorgio, Calvin Klein, Chanel, Yves Saint Laurent. And, as you smelled each one, flat-toned, you told again of not being wanted, your mother's six months trying to abort you. The strawberry birthmark on your chin had been burnt off, since she said it made you even uglier. You told me yet another time how your left hand was tied behind your back at school. How you had to beg for coal, "I had to keep a fire going in the bedroom, my mother so ill one winter." Then you reminded me about the cane your father kept on the scullery wall and — I hadn't heard this part before — the raging slippers he beat the night's *late back, late back,* across your cheeks.

BILATERAL OEDEMA

You didn't understand these words on your final Frailty Report. (Sitting all day in your own home, that one room.) "Just a medical way, Mum, to say both of your legs are swollen with fluid." "Oh, I see…" You couldn't disagree with this one but, as so often, made your own diagnosis: "I think it's my heart causing that…and hairdressing and at the Board*, I was on my legs all day." And they were so swollen. Knotted cords of varicose veins, some of which you'd had removed, but still the kind of legs Lucian Freud might paint: red, blue, black. Huge.

* Seeboard, the electric company.

YOUR CLOTHES

Mostly, your mode of shopping: to buy and buy and then, remembering the nobody you thought you were, the not ever being good enough, the undeserving, the empty-handed pain of lack, you would, after a day or so of defeating indecision, decide "that's too expensive, I'll have to take it back." One of your jobs had dressed you up, then down and out in blue, a uniform, crimplene. Even so, and perhaps because of, all those clothes. Some of them very beautiful. Sixty plastic sacks when they cleared the house. Though for years by then, you always put yourself in black.

WEDDING PHOTOGRAPH

I saw this one every summer in Grandad's front room in a bowed glass cabinet. Your wedding day. The exemplary 1940's bride. Gauze and light over your exuberant hair. Your face expectant, open-eyed. Living downstairs, you kept the photograph by your bedside. And one of your carers exclaimed: "Oh, Mrs D, you were *so* beautiful!" Then the carer asked, "Were you happy?" You told me how the question had made you cry, "I just couldn't help it." In all the years you'd told me about your life, I didn't know about what you said next. And it was typical of you, the way a truth, or so it seemed, came from the blue: a rending fact, tangential, but cataclysmic for the once established, understood. "I was in the doorway at Grandad's, on that brass step, you know, at 176, in my wedding dress and he said to me, "Listen, you don't have to go through with this." Then, as quietly as I've ever heard you speak: "My ol'man did apologise — oh years and years later, a long time after you were born. Whatever else, Lees, it's not just physical, it also wrecks your feelings when someone hits you like my father did. I just had to leave. Wipe Paignton's dust from my feet."

YOUR PERFUMES

You told the pain of your childhood's stories matter of fact, but you didn't know how to stop the surging needs, nor sate black oceans of emptiness. That last Christmas in your own home, you asked me for perfume. I knew by then trying, as always, to dam up the stampeding sea, I'd do anything to get you some. "Which one?" At 89, as precise as ever — sometimes maddeningly so — about sensuous things: "*Youth Dew* by Estée Lauder. In hospital, a young woman with a baby had it on. I passed them going to rehab, after my stroke. The scent was wonderful, gave me hope... ."

BILATERAL OEDEMA

When you tried to stand up the colour of your legs deepened, blood-pressured an angry fat-swell red through both your ankles, feet. "You're lucky, you've got your father's legs... ." And this was true. (When I was young looked good in jeans, just like him). I understood your envy then. Years ago, as things went wrong, you slept on your own in a single bed, "Your father kicks out at night, I won't be able to work, if he hurts my legs." I see you as a seabird in an oil spill. Cold. Wet. Both wings matted black. The waterproofing of your feathers gone.

HYDRANGEAS

Dried and brought inside the house as precursors of winter's sombre rusts: dusk-smudged subtleties. Blushed-blueish through to hard-bruised reds. You called a taxi to take you out, but the carers didn't think you should go. When I agreed with them, you packed your hardest punch: "I don't care what you think, I shouldn't be stopped, you know, it wasn't *me* that was sectioned." Perhaps you'd forgotten what goes around comes around? A few days later, a Sunday afternoon, November, the hospital rang, could I please come? You'd tied a cord around your neck. Together the nurses and I calmed you, put you in your nightdress, swung your immobile legs back into bed. I touched your forehead, said, as you did, so often to me, "God bless". The next day they took you to the psychiatric ward. You were silent, then screaming, leaving your body to put out fires on the sea front, telling me you'd peed on them. But before all this, denying first you'd ever been unkind, you sent me a bouquet. The bouquet made me cry — such beauty. And because you couldn't say, I am so very sorry for what I said. Unusually, on the florist's card, the flowers were all listed: scabies, lysmachia, campanula, clematis, salae and impatiens as if painted in intensity to give proportion to the hurt you caused. And amongst them, all your disparates brought together in one huge, round, white-flowered head. A single stem hydrangea.

MONDAY IN THE PSYCHIATRIC WARD

"Am I dead yet?" You have raised your head from its rag-doll fall. Your white hair, though in delirium, is still thick. From the window in the psychiatric ward, we can't see the incoming tide. Though sometimes smell bladderwrack, salt. My childhood is blue water, Preston Sands, Paignton, sun-streamed rivulets, rock pools, white waves' rushing radiance. And we're both there in the remembering and forgetting of the air. They'd found you in time, untied the cord from around your neck. And now still up close, your face. Which is also not your face. But the beauty in the bright blur of tears as I look, really look, is yours. The ache, mine. Today the wintered Downs are white-dark undulates. The unsayable. Snow-sketched everywhere.

A THURSDAY MORNING

The Downs, green with spring, are sheep-speckled. Despite winter's disavowal, the blackthorn's flowering. Earlier, sitting shoulder-slumped on the edge of your hospital bed— you're sobbing, over and over. "He wasn't buried, he has no grave." The child you lost, before I was born. A miscarriage, sixty years ago. Anguish has become this morning's dark light. I need respite. From the train window, the blackthorn is full on: black, angular spikes and blossom — a fractal, fragile white.

ANOTHER MONDAY

This, too, for Lucian Freud. The way your skin folds, the scale, the tones. The solidity, unmanageability of flesh. Staff stop me in the corridor, Maybe you can help, she won't let any of us go near her. Through the door, against a background of greys, browns, the brush strokes smudged in, smoothed out, your hair's a whirlpool of swirling white. And the sheets in disarray. Bent half-over, you're sitting naked on the bed. The hospital light brunts. The electric air mattress to support your back is flat, you've pulled out the plug. Last time, you told me to bugger off and I went. But, today, the wild bird in you that's caged, the one that scratches, claws and, in your case, even bites, has now, somehow, calmed. I talk you into a cup of tea, get the nurses to get you dressed. In your wheelchair, in the day room, your hair brushed, all but lost among your wanton ramblings, I catch your now-subdued screech of what's going on, "They told me I have to sell the house. I can't ever go back home."

WINGS ARE MADE OF MUSCLE AND BONE

Awkward. I am taking a picture in the middle of the road: on the pedestrian crossing, there's a seagull's wing. And though they're not meant to be in the picture, my feet are there too. In black sandals, new this summer. I've worn them into the care home, as it happens, nearly every time I visit you, it's been so hot. You're usually in bed, stretched out with pillows behind you. The cotton nightdress I gave you gapes at your neck. Since your last stroke, your left hand does nothing and you can't stand up. Sometimes you jerk your legs against your mattress: "Do you think, Lees, I'll ever walk again?"

PAINTINGS

One was just two colours: black and white. White hydrangeas on a black background. You'd had it on a bedroom wall. Though maybe it was done in pastels. The white so soft against the black. One of the best pictures you ever bought and, somehow, shows things I've found so hard to understand. The black and white way you spoke to me as a child. What in therapy I came to call your fiat voice. It flattened me with the wrong I'd done: wanting things I couldn't have. Spelling out, pushing down with too much force. You the adult, me the so young child. And, no doubt, you did have it even worse. But still — all the hards, the unfair, the have-to-be-accepted, impossibilities of, THAT'S LIFE. Strange to say this, since the hydrangeas seem all delicacy in a glass jar. Benign on single stems. Glorious globes. White-frothed, gentle heads.

DENTIST

I catch you first from the back in the waiting room. Your head's slumped forwards, your white hair the giveaway and, even though I see you often, I still brace slightly at the shock. *Shock.* The word takes me to another life: I'm the child, you, the tempestuous one. That evening in the yard, the garden beyond has roses fading in a lime-lit dusk. The game we're playing: the ball's red hot, for god's sake, throw it quickly, use both hands, it mustn't drop. But I let the ball go, bounce away. Running to get it, I trip, smash my mouth on the wall, break my tooth. Terrified, night coming in, summer ending, the darkness of it all, I put myself to bed. I don't suppose, Mum, you remember this? Today, they tilt your wheelchair back, place an awkward cushion for the left-hang of your neck. After your x-ray, there'll be no extraction, just a built-up, pressed-in, rounded off amalgam. Outside, the morning's cool has given way to sun, tempering the blight of browning leaves. You still have your beautiful teeth, though numb now your smile's lopsided. When I was a child, you did call the emergency dentist, but I remember more your fearful yelling, "Christ, what the bloody hell have you done?" Now, on your lap, the hands that picked up the ball are shrunken, faintly freckled, the skin's translucent. While we wait for the taxi to take you back to the care home, I watch carefully, silent, checking you're okay. I can hardly bear to see your fingers twitching. The thinned-out flesh, white bird bone.

THE STATION TO SEVEN DIALS

I want to record this: walking up the hill from the station. Across the road, a man at the corner of the street. I only see him from the back, slow, a stick, a hat. The light — the light, does what? My eyes burn as if there could be no other colour anywhere but black. I'd like to be a painter, paint the man, the softly, shimmered bright that's also, somehow, hard, crystalline. Autumn is already in. A tree ahead of me by the wall has sparse leaves, the limp ones left, cling on. Thin, long with a downward feel, a signal somewhere to their dry-brown scuttle on the ground. Though right now they're also red, resplendent, poised tongues about to speak. But the sun is still too madly-summered, rose-coloured, rose-bled. Mum, you are in all of this of course, though, at first, I didn't know. I simply stared and stared, all the screaming things, far off, far out. I was mesmerised, walking, walking on. In another road, there's still the odd roses proud, upheld on their stems. They know how to stop me short — unfurled, their fevers might begin the down, down into dark. I need words now, ones, you know, for how late roses open out. Two words come: convolute, involute. Will they serve for the muscular, tender petals of the heart?

PAINTINGS

Dad bought another painting for you when I was born. Was it Newquay? I don't know, the surf's not strong. Quintrel Bay, perhaps? I wish I'd kept it now, so do you. Yesterday at the De La Warr Pavilion the rain lashed down, hailed in one of those out-of-nowhere, climate-changed, torrential squalls. I watch the smacking hard of waves. Like the Furies rising up, their uncontrolled hysterias. Though even so, the sea spume's a summer-sunned hydrangea white. The storm-clouds — your diktats — somewhat subdued, still have colour. The background's always there in black. Though I can't hear the waves sound inside the De La Warr. In my ears now, not the force of making me know what we could or couldn't afford, but things we said in the care home I just left. Don't you remember? I've told you (again and again) Mum, (my hand, a flower I hope, on your arm) the house is sold. Had to be… We've got to pay, pay the fees. Some days you get it all — the Quintrel sea's a greeny, bluey, subtle grey, the waves, that lapping kind of calm — though yesterday you didn't. Your so small voice echoes and empties me: "Are there still those paintings on my walls?"

WINGS ARE MADE OF MUSCLE AND BONE

Your face is bright, alive with the possible flight to horizons since, even in storm — I see it in your eyes — you believe over the sea's blue somewhere, there's still a flash-flood of sunlight. "Mum, your hair looks nice, the way the nurses have gripped it back." The photo I've taken this unreasonably warm October on the pedestrian crossing is mostly white stripe — the white of your perennial summer jacket. The white of two designer bags I found buried in clothes under the stairs. The white of your hair. The white of the low tide's lapping ordinance. And there's an inexplicable smudge of white on the tarmac too. Not the white of the care home's sheet, but the kind which might be paint daubed energetically on a portrait. Looking at the photo, I also imagine I have found your doppy shoes and the crossing's black stripe a long walk off. And your wings aren't lying there air-crashed, bone-smashed, muscle-wasted.

OCTOBER

The sky, a cooling blue. On the rowan tree outside your window in the care home, clusters of red berries forecast, it's said, a hard, incoming chill. Half-slumped in your wheelchair, your white hair's feathered thin around your face. The rest's gripped back and, though you're fatter than I've ever seen you, your pale eyes widen and, despite cataracts, still brim with summer. I'd like to paint colours for the care home, us, this afternoon — render the mood. Hopper-style? And then follow the advice we were given about a bird trapped once in our sitting room: shade the room, open the window, close the door to leave, saying, as if you were that bird (mad as this hope is) "Mum, before the winter comes you will, somehow, find your own way out."

PNEUMONIA

Fast-gasp breathing. Head slumped down. Through the oxygen mask you're trying to speak. Your mouth gaping. Soundless. Shoulders heaving. "Your mother's infection markers are sky-high." The doctor's preparing me. "There's a large patch on the x-ray." Where the mind goes…meaning, metaphor? Pneumonia, *Pneuma:* wind, spirit, God's breath. My hand on your head. "Get some rest." Your hand, a wrinkling blood-bruise, a tangled net of needles, swabs, transparent tubes. Trying to tell me something, pressing your palms together. Laying them on the side of your head, eyes closing. Do you want to die? Live? A Paignton girl at prayer? Bible left lost in the old white wardrobe, brown-paper cover, date of confirmation 1938, never knowing you as 'Janeta'… Short, shallow, rhythmic gasping. Dad, dying, pneumonia too, pulling at the mask "Take it off! Take it off!" those trees then, a green swathe, early morning, low, swaying. And now you're trying. Trying. Still you're trying… A bird. Shoulder-heaving. Wingless. On water. Every which way *hospital* written on your nightdress in small letters. Drowning. Every which way, every which colour, a child's exercise for the right hand, the other, behind your back, tied, school nights screaming, now underwater, hospital, hospital, hospital, your clouded eyes, drowning. "I have to leave so you get some rest." Deep-sea drowning. Such white hair, your hair. A wheezing, mask-whispered, breath-bubbled "God bless…" At the main exit heart-holding, a bird in the wind wavers. Steadies. Then the bird, the bird you are, swerves up. Up. Out of the water. Up into the long-lung'd, long-lived air.

BROKEN IMAGES

I am cycling at the gym. On the TV, Japanese girls taking a selfie. Their red lips pout, blow kisses into blossoming cherry trees, white again, for another spring. White. With the look of flowers that are looked at. Earlier, in A&E* yet again, your eyes, red-rimmed, perceive hard landscapes, don't recognise me. Forgetful snow has given way to this. "She was daddy's girl" you say as I take your hand, "You do look like her." "But, Mum, it is me!" Your unwashed hair falls lank, your talk's a disconnect, "I pushed him in the car." On your wrist a gauze swathe. Hanging loose, a long tube from the bag of liquid antibiotics for your veins. You've ripped off the heart monitor. Now it pulses too fast, beats red alarm. Unseeing, you gaze into stale air. "His blood was on my denim jacket." The trees offer no hiding place. The sky, no grace. "Would you like to see his grave?" The doctor wheels in a machine to find kidneys, gallbladder and, of course, your heart. He wants to gain your trust, "I'm just trying to find out what's wrong with you..." Puts a cold gel on your chest, then a metal disc. You hiss, fight him off, "Leave me be!" "Doctor," I should've said, "draw up closer, closer to where the roots clutch. Come with me, I will show you something. Guilt in the dust." The gym's deserted, the programme, still Japan. I push harder on the bike's pedals as two more girls in pinafores throw petals skyward. Light, the sunned-drift-down of blossom. My wheels go round. I am where I am. Black weights in the gym do not lift.

---

* Accident and Emergency (ER, Emergency Room)

PREPARATION

For a death. Yours. How to do such a thing? There are, of course, the forms. Wishes written down, ticked boxes, then coffined away in the care home's office. Last July I walked along the same Brighton Streets we always walked to the Saturday market. Past the terraced houses where you wished you lived, to the "off-beat-something-different" shops and, on one doorway hanging up outside the long, orange silk duster coat I fell in love with, bought, then brought into the care home. "What do you think, Mum?" You were better than you are today, when you are here a moment, then seeing lace over a door, marked down at fifteen pounds. As if on stage your madness, Ophelia's; your white hair, Lear's. Dark all around you, a spotlight on your face, then a shift in your voice so quiet, eerie — a blurred-eye luminosity such that the audience is rapt withal. The nurse called me in and with broken English said, "No funeral plan in place, better you do now.' Not to be resuscitated. Cremated. Though I'm sure, if it had been on the form, you would've chosen a Brighton terrace. And, if in one of your raging swings, thunder, lightning, a blasted heath.

AT THE SUPERMARKET

It's something like this: I stop to look at the fish through the counter's glass. They've been put out carefully on chipped chunks of ice. I would like to paint the fish or shape them some other way, call the work: *At the Fish Market — Detail*. I visited a fish market once in Portugal, the platonic form: striped stall awnings, abundant green, black, tigered mackerel, rubber-fubble of squid. And so many fish I didn't recognise. And somehow you were there: fish as jewels — the precious rings you loved. You'd taught me about platinum, silver, gold, the different carats and their stones: amethyst, sapphire, ruby, emerald, and your favourite, cold-eyed diamond. I often saw them pushed into tight black velvet slits, shown off in a lockable glass cabinet. The same cabinet I unearthed in the garage, the day the man came to price the house in order to clear it. Cold, wrapped in black, emptied of your sparkle, all those glittering, pretty things. And there on the supermarket counter, bream are laid out in layers, open-mouthed, almost as if singing. I cannot look away. The mesmerising silvers, smooth scales, gold-ringed, black-centred eyes, their blunt, curved heads — sculpture-cold. The music for a requiem.

EVERY SO OFTEN ALONG MANOR ROAD

hanging over walls, the red lanterns of fuchsia with long, delicate, inner filaments, all those years ago. The road stilled in sun-cut heat, gulls, and our slow, sauntering steps away from sea-sand days at the beach. Had I really forgotten what we called *the popping flowers*, starred red and purpling when open and before that, though, a pod almost plastic to the touch? I don't know. But when my husband brought a straggled clutch of fuchsia in from the rain yesterday, somehow you were there in your blue towelling robe, your tanned and freckled shoulders gleaming with oil, beach-mats under your arm and I knew again the smell of salt on an inland wind, and how I'd seen your father in the cool interior of his house, fallen drunk. But this is too conscious now. The damp flowers I put in a glass jar, held all this without words, a kind of interfuse of things, and my fingers on their own, with the ease of expertise found the perfect pressure to release the fuchsia's popping sound. My hand, a child's. My mind, all those summers backlit by the lamps of time.

THE BIRD YOU ARE

Is summer in a rose garden. Is hanging out sheets. Is a redhead in a turquoise raincoat. Is red lipstick. Is the high blue sky. Is singing. Is splashing through waves on Preston beach. Is soothing vinegar on my sunburnt leg. Is squawking and squawking. Is packing a case on Christmas Day to leave for good. Is back by the gas fire, crying, polishing. Is bagging the boot-fair's fruit. Is hitting a police woman. Is cataract-blind. Is two hands' push on the commode's sides. Is unable to fly. Is "Next time you visit, dear, bring acid." Is tying a cord around her neck. Is a hoist in the care home. Is ravaged. Is drugged. Is tattered feathers. Is such white hair. Is head-hanging heavy over a low-slung branch. Is tarred at the feathered edge. Is at the school gates hovering, turquoise in soft rain-sun-dazzling. Is flying into our garden's June scent, the sheets whitened in the wind of remembering.

ACKNOWLEDGMENTS AND APPRECIATIONS

I am very grateful to everyone in two poetry groups who read these prose poems, one by one, over the time of writing: Peter Abbs, Colin Bell, Patrick Bond, Julian Broughton, Wendy French, Angela Kirby, Kim Lasky, Paul Matthews, Kay Syrad, Ann Williams, and Patricia Wooldridge.

The very positive responses, as well as the thoughtful comments I received, were hugely encouraging, especially as I was writing these prose poems in the last and very difficult years of my mother's life.

I am also very appreciative of other readers for their helpful editorial suggestions and very positive comments as the manuscript came closer to its final form: Nigel Butler, Alistair Davies, Jane Mogford, Stella Skordalellesis, and Ann Wroe.

Huge thanks, too, to Andrea Hollander, Patricia Wooldridge, Kim Lasky, and Kay Syrad, for reading the final manuscript and giving it their generous endorsements.

I would also like to thank Annette De Mestre for her suggestion of the image for the front cover.

Finally, I am immensely grateful to Gemma Whelan and Adam Liberman of Shangana Press for deciding to publish my work. Adam, thank you too, for everything you have done preparing the manuscript.

PREVIOUS PUBLICATIONS

'Every So Often Along Manor Road' was first published in *Eastern Iowa Review* (Issue 10, Spring 2020).

'Pneumonia' (as 'Mercury, and Even So My Mother') was first published in *Tears in the Fence* (2019).

'The Bird You Are' (as 'My Mother') and 'Edward Hopper's Picture of You' (as 'Hopper's Picture of My Mother') were first published in *Envoi* (2019).

ABOUT THE AUTHOR

Lisa Dart is a poet and prose writer. A finalist for the Grolier Poetry Prize (USA, 2004), The Aesthetica Poetry Competition (UK, 2013), and The Troubadour International Poetry Prize (UK, 2022), she has a doctorate in creative writing from the University of Sussex (UK). Her poetry has appeared in many journals, including *Eastern Iowa Review*, *Tears in The Fence*, and *The London Magazine*. She is the author of *The Linguistics of Light* (poems, Salt, 2008); *Fathom* (prose memoir, Free Association Press, 2019); *This Thing of Darkness* (IPBooks, 2024), a highly experimental illustrated book using multiple texts, which won a British Arts Council Award; and *Even So, This Song* (Shangana Press, 2025).

www.ingramcontent.com/pod-product-compliance
Lightning Source LLC
Chambersburg PA
CBHW011225120626
46545CB00010B/3159